By
Darren Carter

Waterfall
of
Dreams

To order additional copies of this book, contact:
Xlibris
0800-056-3182
www.xlibrispublishing.co.uk
Orders@ Xlibrispublishing.co.uk

ISBN: Softcover   978-1-9845-9475-4
            EBook   978-1-9845-9476-1

Print information available on the last page

Rev. date: 04/21/2020

Table of Contents

Dancing Demons

Dancing around the fire of hell.
Dancing demons dance,
As mankind fails.

Every time you sin on earth.
The dancing demons know your true worth.

The dancing demons dance with delight.
As their master has claimed another soul tonight.

Beautiful Songbird

Sing me to my dreams.
As I lay by the crystal stream.
Sing me to my hearts love.
Sing me to heaven above.

You take me on a journey of beauty,
In the arms of loves destiny.

Beautiful songbird,
You sing a sweet melody.
Take me to loves mystery.

Kingdom of Hope

In a kingdom of hope.
Lived a king in heavenly love.
He did good deeds for his people every day.
The people loved him,
In so many different ways.

Every day,
They honoured his name.
When enemies waged war.
The men of the kingdom came.

He was their protector.
He was their teacher.
He loved telling the children,
Stories of the magic bell.

It would ring in time of danger.
It would ring when the king summoned his royal messenger.

It would ring on a wedding day.
To send the loving couple on their way.
But today the bell rings with sadness.
As the old king has left us.
The kingdom is in mourning.
The children are crying.

Happiness soon returns.
As the heir to his throne has been crowned.
The people are happy once more.
As the king's son,
has made the kingdom glorious as it was before.

Basset Hound

A Bassett Hound.
I'm homeward bound.
I've been around the town,
With my master.
He's a Primary School Teacher.

I love going for a walk in the park.
I love to bark.
We play throw and catch.
Then I meet my friend Patch.

We go off exploring.
While our masters are talking.
The park is our domain.
We love it in the rain.

We roll about on the grass.
Which makes our masters,
Smile and laugh.
Then it's time to go home.
So I can have my bone.

Dandy Lion

Butterflies and Bumblebees,
Take their rest on me.
They stop for a chat.
I am a comedian.
I make them laugh.

The other wild flowers,
Have heard my jokes so many times before.
But it doesn't stop them,
Laughing at them even more.

Mother Nature,
The goddess of life.
When she hears my jokes,
Makes her laugh.

I take her tears away.
As she sometimes has a bad day.

Mr Tweak

I am Mr Tweak.
I appear when you write.
I come out,
When it doesn't seem right.

I am your corrector.
I make your words sound better.
The point you needed to express.
I, Mr Tweak,
Have sorted out your little mess.

King of Scrabble

The jungle will rumble,
When the lion wakes up.
The animals are scared,
They run to the hill tops.

The lion is free in the jungle.
He is looking for someone to play scrabble.
He is the king of the board.
It stops him from getting bored.

Being such a great success.
The other animals have lost interest.
The animals don't find joy in scrabble anymore.
As the lion always wins,
Then he roars.

Fairy Elephant

An elephant called Lucy.
She was being quite silly.
She always wanted to be a fairy.
So her mother made her a dress.
She was her mother's little princess.

Lucy had golden wings.
She would also try to sing.
But when she sang,
She was out of tune.
But she carried on,
Because in her world she was perfection.

Lucy imagined,
Flying in the sky.
Lucy imagined,
Granting all the other animals their wishes.
At the end of the day.
Her mother would cover her with loving kisses.

To Dream a Dream

To dream a dream,
When love is true.
To dream a dream,
Your heart knew.

To dream a dream,
Of a love so young.
To dream a dream,
Your heart belonged.

The Dawn

The dawn of a new day.
The birds sing songs of the month of May.
The season of Spring and Summer,
Bring the cheers of the end of Autumn and Winter.

The veil of white snow,
Is now a beautiful meadow.
The trees with their leaves,
When Autumn came they were blown away by its breeze.

Mother Nature was asleep,
In the cold months of Winter.
Now she's awake.
But in her dreams,
She will always remember.

The Warlock

Under lock and key.
I hide from the Warlock,
As he searches for me.

With witchcraft and spells.
He knows the dark art well.
The witches are his Coven.
They come from Salem.

He calls many manifestations.
From the realm of damnation.
The angel of death shall come,
On a steed of night.
If you catch its sight.
It will take what you hold most dear.
Your soul,
I fear.

Natures Whisper

Natures whisper,
The wind is what you hear.
Invisible to the eye.
You know it's there.
As it blows through your hair.

Natures whisper,
The touch of Mother Nature.
Blows away the season of Winter,
And brings in the gentle breeze of Summer.

The Trojan Horse

Under a foreign sun.
Men came to a kingdom of sand and stone.
They built a horse,
From the wood of trees.
To bring a kingdom finally to its knees.

When Troy fell asleep.
Greek warriors escaped from the wooden horse,
And ran through the streets.
Destroying a kingdom,
Which stood for a thousand years.
As destiny cried tears.

Weeping Willow

The Weeping Willow,
Has so much sorrow.
The Weeping Willow,
Has a friend in a little Sparrow.

The Sparrow sings beautiful songs to the Willow tree.
Which makes it very happy.

Mother Nature knows,
When the little Sparrow goes.
The Weeping Willow will be weeping with sorrow.
Till the little Sparrow returns tomorrow.

Black Bear

A black bear,
Wakes from its Winter's sleep.
Now he's hungry,
He needs to eat.

He goes to the river to catch fish.
He has only one wish.
To catch enough fish,
To feed his great appetite.
Then he will sleep all through the night.

Now he's eaten all his fish.
He has another wish.
To go to bed.
As his tummy is well fed.

Jokers in the Pack

The Jokers in the pack.
Make all the other cards laugh.
They are great friends.
Their friendship shall never end.

They go together like strawberries and cream.
They are a double act,
Supreme.

The red Joker is the straight man.
The blue Joker is the fool.
He made the other cards laugh so much,
They fell off the stool.

When they are put away.
You can still hear the jokes they say.
The laughter is now a whisper.
Because it is at night.
As the Dolls are in their beds,
Warm and tight.

Ivory Tower

In an ivory tower,
Awake every hour.
There's an old man.
Counting all his money.
This makes the old man very happy.

This gives him his meaning to his life.
He buys expensive jewels for his wife.

Outside his world is another.
Where the people are a lot poorer.
They struggle.
They shed tears.
They don't have happy days.
They don't have happy years.

One night,
An Owl flies to the window and tells the old man of their sorrow.

The Owl says,
"They will be your friend.
If you bring their poverty to its end.
You have the power to do this.
Grant them this wish."

The Owl asks again.
"Do you want a friend?"
The old man replies,
"Yes!"

The old man soon finds,
Friendship is the best.

Nightingale

The Nightingale,
Loves to sing.
To thank Mother Nature for everything.
She is so grateful.
That Mother Nature is so beautiful.

Mother Nature,
Blows her a kiss and has only one wish.
That the Nightingale,
Of nature's beauty.
Always sing songs,
To waken the days destiny.

Miss Evelyn Gates

Miss Evelyn Gates,
Never hates.
She loves to be good.
She lives in a cottage in the woods.

She knows of natural remedies,
Which she uses to cure.
When the animals are hurt,
They call for her.

Miss Evelyn Gates,
Is a white witch of the woods.
She would cast a white spell on the world,
For it to be good.

She lives in perfect harmony with Mother Nature.
All the creatures love her.

Snowflake

In the Winter's gaze.
A snowflake falls from heavens grace.
It lives upon natures wind.
Which came from the worlds end.

It only exists for a time.
Then in a blink of an eye,
It disappears.
Mother Nature's frozen tears.

Promises

From a true heart,
They came to be.
A true promise has its own destiny.
Out of love,
They were given.
A promise made from heaven.

Tambourine Jane

Tambourine Jane,
She loves her name.
She loves writing songs,
She does this all day long.

Tambourine Jane,
Dances in the rain.
She is a creature of habit.
She has a pet rabbit.

Tambourine Jane,
She has a tender heart.
She loves playing her tambourine and her harp.

Tambourine Jane,
Wishes she was an angel.
As she is so kind and gentle.

Jungle Fever

There's jungle fever,
In the jungle tonight.
All the animals are having a party,
Under the moonlight.

The Hyena is laughing.
The lion is roaring.
All the monkeys are in the trees.
The birds are singing to the Bumblebees.

No predator or prey.
Just perfect harmony this day.
All the animals are one.
Till the jungle sun comes at dawn.

Dessert Factory

Our dessert factory has gone berserk.
A gremlin has got into the works.

It can't stop making desserts,
Day and night.
From forest gateau to angel delight.

If it's not stopped.
The world will be in trouble.
It will look from outer space.
Like a huge raspberry ripple.

The children have stopped the gremlin from all its meddling.
Now the children begin to do all the eating.

When Mother Nature Calls

All the animals answer her call.
From the very great to the very small.
They listen to the words she speaks.
They touch the hearts of the strong and weak.

The animals are governed by her sun and her moon.
They know when it's the day.
They know when it's the night.
They know when to eat.
They know when to fight.

Mother Nature,
Bestows gifts.
To be swift.
To be cunning.
To be strong.
To know no wrong.

Animals of nature.
Are as innocent as she.
As Mother Nature does what needs to be.

The Church Bell

At every hour.
The church bell rings in the tower.
A church made from stone.
It stands on the hill all alone.

Looking over the town below,
Is its way of saying hello.

Temple of the Four Winds

In a secret place,
Of stone and ice.
Lies a temple of gold,
Of ancient grace.

The keepers here,
Keep watch day and night.
The guard the four winds of magical delight.

When the winds have shown to the world their power.
They return at the midnight hour.

They are all strong and powerful.
But when they leave the temple,
One remains.
The gentle wind,
Which comes after the rain.

She is young and youthful.
She makes the world beautiful.

She is the breeze,
Which touches your cheek on a Summers day.
She is the breeze which blows your sail,
And shows you the way.
She is there when you say your last goodbye.
She is the breath of an angel of the sky.

Good Luck Charm

Good luck charm,
You bring me joy.
I have had you,
Since I was a boy.

You've been in my family,
As long as I can remember.
You were given to me by my father.
You have been passed down to every generation.
Now, I am your next destination.

I will use you in Vegas,
On the roulette table.
Lucky charm you will not fail.

I will break the bank.
You shall be the one I shall thank.

Cat Nap

I think it's time for a snooze.
But first I need to blow my nose.

I feel so tired.
I could sleep forever.
Or at least till my dinner.

My home is nice and warm.
But I can hear the Winters storm.

I will be like,
Sleeping beauty.
But I hope a handsome prince doesn't disturb me.

It is my nap time.
I look forward to this every day.
When I close my eyes,
I shall be away.

Dreamland

In a blissful sleep.
Where dreams are born.
Dreamland exists,
For the young and old.

A world of magic and wonder.
You will never be scared,
As there is no sound of the thunder.

The old,
Dream of ages past.
Where their love was true,
And it would forever last.

It is such a beautiful place.
The children always sleep,
With a smile on their face.

Flash of Lightning

Flash of lightning.
The thunder breaks.
The earth feels your power and it shakes.

I gaze at you from my window.
You light up the sky with your wonder.
The world hears your thunder.

The coming of the rain.
The raindrops fall again and again.

The storm is here in the sky.
I can see it with my eyes.

The wonder of Mother Nature,
Is here tonight.
What a wonderful sight.

The Scent of the Rose

Mother Nature's sweet whisper.
A moment to remember.
A breeze of sweetness on the air.
The scent of the rose of love,
She wished to share.

Mother Nature walks alone.
Her daughters of life have all left home.
She watches from her tower of stone.
The beautiful world she calls her own.

Her love she shows,
Is in the beauty of the rose.
She wished the world to see.
The love she has for you and me.

Stormy Weather

The eye of the storm,
Watches the world below.
With its rain and hail.
Its saying hello.

Stormy weather.
The weather of Winter.
The ice and snow.
Hides secrets,
Only heaven knows.

Run inside.

Where shelter lies,

And watch the stormy weather from the skies.

Dear Father Christmas

"Dear Father Christmas,
This is Jimmy.
I can't wait for you to come down our chimney.

All our stockings are waiting for you,
For Christmas Day.
I hope you don't lose your way.

Charlie,
Will be about.
He won't bark or bite.
As he will be in his bed,
Warm and tight.

Please, take a seat.
Put your feet up and rest.
As you Father Christmas are the very best.
From Jimmy."

Bed of Dreams

I climb the stairs,
To my bed of dreams.
I sleep a sleep of angels.
I hear the angels sing.

This dreamland,
Is a place for girls and boys.
There is an abundance of joys.

A treasure chest full of beauty,
For your eyes delight.
It is always there,
When you sleep at night.

Weather Machine

A mad Scientist has gone around the twist.
He wants to hold the whole world to ransom.
In his ice - cold kingdom.
He has created a weather machine.
He wishes the world to be white not green.

He wants the world to be covered in snow.
He wants the icy winds to forever blow.

Every day,
Every night.
The cold winds he created will forever bite.

Mother Nature cries,
As she gazes towards the sunrise.
The sun shines on the veil of white.
She wishes the world to be beautiful and bright.

But even with her sun,
She can't mend the damage he has done.

Mysterious

I'm heading to the town Mysterious.
Are you superstitious?
It is where ghosts and ghouls dwell.
They are hiding out from hell.

When the poor,
Long lost traveller enters the town.
Everywhere is peaceful,
There is no sound.

When the old church bell rings the hour of midnight.
Every creepy being comes alive.
They rejoice,
Especially on this night.
As its Halloween.
It is time for everyone to scream.

The Storm

The sky welcomes the clouds of the storm.
The heavy rain falls,
Stay dry in your homes.

When the thunder and lightning strike.
You will be safe,
Inside your homes tonight.

The rain falls from the skies.
When Mother Nature's anger dies.
The rainbow will rise.

When You Cry

When you cry.
The angels in heaven have tears in their eyes.
They descend from heaven,
Their blessed haven.

To bring you songs of perfect happiness.
To take away your tears of sadness.

They bring you heavenly love and kindness.
As they were created from Gods holiness.

Magic

Magic the cat.
Sits on the table by the Witches hat.
The witch comes in.
She is naughty like sin.

She strokes Magic on his head.
She yawns,
As its time for bed.
She places her broom by the door.
She gives it orders to sweep the floor.

When she is in her warm bed.
She scratches her head.
She thinks of new spells she can create.
To make the land have fear and shake.

When the new day comes.
She feeds Magic,
As he has a hungry tum.

When night comes.
She orders the broom to come to her hand.
Then she flies all over the land.

Winterland

As the snow falls.
Games are played by all the girls and boys.
The Winterland,
Where the army of Snowmen stand.

They watch the white flakes of snow fall from the sky.
There's excitement in the children's eyes.

The season of joy is here.
As Christmas Day is getting nearer.

Christmas Trees,
The sign of the season.
Waiting for Santa Claus to bring presents for all the children.

The Mountain of Natures Dream

The veil of white,
Covers the land.
It's a fairy tale made from love.
A beautiful gift,
Given by heaven above.

A stairway to the sky.
Where the angels of heaven fly.
Beauty lives here.
Mother Nature is near.

A magical place.
Where Mother Nature shows her grace.
The coldness of her touch,
Puts life in an eternal sleep.
Till Spring returns with its haze and heat.

Wise Old Man

Far away in a distant land.
Lives a wise old man.

From his pen,
Stories are born.
They are given life,
When they are read in your homes.

At bedtime,
When children are ready to sleep.
His stories are read,
They bring sweet dreams.

His stories will always live in the world.
As they are for children,
Who see the gift of his words.

Left Outside in the Dark

Left outside in the dark.
The only sound I can hear,
Is a dog's bark.
The shadows scare me.
The cold wind greets me.
She wants me to follow her.
I can't resist.
Her cold wind gives me a reassuring kiss.

I look back where I was sitting.
I feel a cold shiver.
I begin to cry.
I wonder why?

The whole place has no face.
A bell chimes for heavenly grace.
Then I wake from my nightmare.
But when I know where I am.
It brings me joy not fear.
As I know my parents are near.

Fairies Kisses

In the enchanted wood.
Where Mother Nature caresses the trees,
With her cool breeze.

Fairies dwell,
By the old wishing well.
They lead you to your wish.
When you receive it,
They give you a gentle kiss.

A kiss of innocence.
You will always believe in their existence.

You walk away,
With love in your heart this day.
Love will always lead the way.

Death of a Fairy Tale

The beautiful sun has gone.
The magic of the kingdom,
Was stolen.
No more wishes in the wishing well.
This is the death of a fairy tale.

The angels in heaven heard the fairy tales cries.
They came to her,
With tears in their eyes.
They touched the fairy tale,
With heavenly love.
The darkness fled away,
To the skies above.

Cuthbert and Herbert

Cuthbert the teddy bear,
Loves his liquorice and sherbet.
He shares it with his friend Herbert.

When you see one,
You see the other.
They are always together.
You could call them brothers.

Cuthbert and Herbert,
Love their sweet treat.
It makes them happy,
All the way down to their feet.

Now it's time to play.
Here comes Faye.
She has come home from school.
She left Cuthbert and Herbert sitting on the stool.

Angels Watching Over Me

Angels watching over me while I sleep.
My dreams are touched by their grace.
When I wake,
I have a smile on my face.

When I dream.
I dream of beauty.
I dream of worlds of fantasy.
These angels unlock the mystery.
They are Guardians.
It's their sacred duty.

I feel safe in my bed.
No nightmares threaten me.
As I have my angels watching over me.

74

Atlas

In a universe of stars,
Our galaxy lies.
Atlas holds up our planet,
Hidden from our eyes.

He was found guilty of his crimes.
Now Zeus orders him,
To hold up our planet for the rest of time.

The Magic is Gone

"The magic is gone!"
The Wizard cried.

"The gift has escaped.
Now I hide my face within my cape.
It was given to me by the Enlighten One.
Now it has escaped and run.

I used it for evil,
Rather for good.
I was warned that my gift would;
Disappear if it could.

Now it's gone.
I am no magic one.
Will it ever return to me?
I have learnt my lesson.
I can't be without my magic power.
As emptiness will haunt me every hour.

Come back to me,
Magic power.
I am so empty.
I am so sorry."

Kingdom of Glory

In the enchanted forest,
Long ago.
Stood a kingdom of glory.
It stood against the darkness of fury.

Day and night.
The fury came to destroy.

The kingdom of glory,
Would never lie in ruin.
As its walls were built by angels of heaven.

It had the power of the Light of heaven.
It would never be beaten.

The fury,
Finally gave in.
The Light shone within.
The fury,
Became good.
As the angels in heaven knew he would.
Now they live in perfect harmony.
One honours the day.
One honours the night.
They only speak,
When its twilight.

Night of Dreams

Night of dreams.
A time to believe.
Where the mystery and fantasy lie.
When tiredness closes your eyes.

Dreams of beauty,
Live in the echo of destiny.
The mind will see,
What the night of dreams wishes.
A thousand and one kisses.

Blessings come.
When you say your prayers.
The night of dreams,
Will keep nightmares at bay.

As the night of dreams,
Wishes you to have fun and joy.
When you wake,
There is happiness.
With every girl and boy.

Supernatural

From another time.
From another place.
These spirits,
are shy to show their face.

They hide in the shadows.
They make no sound.
But you sense that they are around.

When they appear.
They bring fear.
Your heart beats even faster.
Especially when you feel a cold hand on your shoulder.

So always stay in the light.
It will protect you from a terrible fright.

To Shed a Tear

To shed a tear.
The cries of sadness.
Each tear,
Is a memory of sadness of your heart.
The angels of heaven,
Also cry.
While they play their harps.

Angel Tears

Angel tears fall like gentle rain.
They feel your sadness.
They feel your pain.

God wipes their tears away.
He sends them to the sadness of yesterday.
Where His Son was crucified.
It was a sacrifice,
He was willing to die.

Day and Night

The day loves the night.
The night loves the day.
Long lost lovers,
Where love will find a way.

It comes with the eclipse.
An eternal kiss.
A wish which comes,
When the moon is full.
A sight made from love,
So wonderful.

Tomorrow

Tomorrow,
Never bring me any sorrow.
Let there be happiness,
Never sadness.
Let it last,
Till the day turns to night.
Then I will thank,
God for the day.
With all my might.

Humble Pie

I'm eating humble pie.
It gives you time to think,
What you did wrong.

The more you eat.
The more you see the picture,
And why you were punished by your teacher.

"I was only having fun.
I'm a kid,
I am young.
It was a mistake,
I will never do again.
As I wasn't allowed to play out all weekend."

Autumn Leaves

The Autumn leaves,
Hold onto the memory of Summer.
Of times when we were all happy.
The breeze takes them upon the wind.
Where it takes them,
Will be their journeys end.

The Autumn leaves,
Know the secrets of the sunrise.
Natures beauty never dies.

Gingerbread Men

Gingerbread men,
Small and sweet.
You are nice to eat.

Gingerbread men,
Small and sweet.
You are a nice afternoon treat.

Gingerbread men,
You bring the family together.
When we eat you,
We all feel a lot better.

Birds Song

From the heavens,
The birds sing.
It's time to close your eyes to dream.

Since the world was first born.
Birds have sung their beautiful songs.

Fallen angels from the sky.
They sing beautiful songs to mankind.
A perfect lullaby.

The Troll

There was once a Troll,
Long ago.
Who lived under a bridge,
Because he had nowhere else to go.

At night he would gaze at the stars so bright,
And thank the Gods for his life.

No one dared to cross the bridge during the day.
They would wait for the hour of midnight.
When the Troll was dreaming dreams of beautiful delight.

Mr Can't Decide

Black or white.
Fat or thin.
Mr Can't Decide,
Can't decide on anything.

To be asleep,
Or awake.
The decision,
Gives Mr Can't Decide a headache.

Mr Can't Decide,
Needs a voice of reason in his ear.
It will make his world a lot clearer.

Little Princess

Little Princess,
Beautiful and good.
You live in an enchanted wood.

You love to touch the trees.
Mother Nature kisses you with her breeze.
You adore natures flowers.
You love nature in the morning hours.

In a castle,
You dream of love.
A handsome Prince,
Sent to you from heaven above.

You sit by your bedroom window and dream the day away.
Dreaming of your wedding day.

Mr Tumbleweed

Mr Tumbleweed lives in the trees.
He suffers from hay fever,
Which makes him sneeze.

Living in the woods.
Living in the trees.
Mr Tumbleweed eats honey,
Made from the honeybee.

Mr Tumbleweed,
Is green and made from the leaves of every tree.
He is never sad.
He is always happy.

Mr Tumbleweed,
Is very shy.
If he wasn't with the trees.
It would make him cry.

The Ferryman

The Ferryman takes me across the River Styx.
I have paid my fare,
Now I feel so scared.

The Ferryman takes me towards the sound of sorrowful cries.
To a place where heaven is hidden from my eyes.

I have done much wrong.
Now with Hades,
Is where I belong.

Those Dancing Feet

I've got those dancing feet.
I'm dancing to the groovy beat.
Life seems so good,
When I'm in this mood.

I can feel the rhythm,
From my head to my feet.
I do love this groovy,
Crazy beat.

Oswald the Whale

Oswald the whale likes telling tales.
He likes getting the other whales in trouble.
As he is a bit of a rebel.

When Oswald sleeps.
He snores so bad.
Which keeps the other whales awake.
Which makes their parents mad.

Oswald the whale,
Loves eating fish.
He would eat them all day,
If he had his wish.

Oswald the whale,
Knows the tales of the Ocean.
His mother has told him stories of the God Neptune.

Happy Stranger

"Happy Stranger.
Why are you happy?"

"I have just won the lottery.
Now the world is my oyster.
All the dreams I can buy for my daughter.
There's nothing I can't buy.
All I needed was lady luck to be by myside."

Pool of Forever

Gaze at the reflection of destiny.
It holds the mystery.
To behold paradise,
Is a pleasure for the eyes.
The spirit is taken by the crystal waters.
It refreshes the soul.
It brings it to the eternal.

The Dark Night

The dark night.
When phantoms and ghouls come out to fright.
Children beware.
Never be caught unaware.
They are out to get you.
To take you to their domain.
Where the sun doesn't shine,
And there is no rain.

Summer is Over

Summer is over.
It marks the coming of Winter.
When the animals gather,
And the trees begin to slumber.
Mother Nature,
Kisses the Summer season goodbye.
Autumn prepares natures lullaby.
Summer leaves a promise.
That when Spring begins,
Summer will be here when the birds sing.

Mr and Mrs Cuckoo

Mrs Cuckoo is going around the twist.
As she hasn't cleaned her nest,
For her visitor arriving at half past six.

Mr Cuckoo is still in bed.
He is a lazy head.

"All the other birds are wide awake.
Why are you giving me such a headache.
You need to get up.
I've got things to do.
Why don't you go out and find some food for us two?"

Duvet Day

Duvet day.
No school for me today.
I am having a lie in.
My father is doing the shopping.

I wonder,
Will I get my breakfast in bed?
I am so cosy.
I have a sleepy head.

The weekend is here.
I am going to have so much fun.
My breakfast has arrived,
I'm having a fried bacon bun.

The Magic Clock

Hear the chime.
The magical time.
The magic clock is unlocked.

Your destiny is the key.
You can go back when it all began.
Or go forward,
To see the future of man.

The world of time is your domain.
Time for you will never be the same.

Gypsy Queen

Gypsy Queen,
A heavenly delight.
You dance under the magical moonlight.

With your mystical charms and powers.
You tell me my future in this promised hour.

A long life,
Love and fortune.
A promise made under the magical moon.

Lonely Wind

Lonely wind,
Without a friend.
You blow your wind without an end.

From the North you go.
To blow your wind throughout the world.

Mother Nature is always there.
Please,
Don't feel the demon of loneliness and despair.

Happy Charlie

Happy Charlie.
Is a happy cat and that is that.

He loves to purr.
He loves to lick his fur.
He loves his cream.
He loves to dream.

He loves being in the garden.
It's his own little Eden.
He watches life go by.
Then he goes to sleepy bye.

Dream Catcher

Beware of the Dream Catcher.
It's a shy creature.
No one has ever seen it.
As it runs so fast.
It looks for dreams which will last.

When you are asleep in your beds.
He places its small hands on your heads.

He looks inside your mind,
And sees a dream.
It makes him giggle.
He says his riddle.

"Dream a dream for me.
I wish to see.
I will take it as my own.
As happiness hasn't touched this heart of stone."

When you wake,
And you can't remember your dream.
It's been stolen.
Never feel heartbroken.

The Dream Catcher is happy.
He will be like a busy bee.
Now he will take my dream from me.

Waterfall of Dreams

The waterfall of dreams.
Where the Fairies of the woods go.
It's their secret place,
Only Mother Nature knows.

The calm of the water,
Makes the Fairies remember.
The wishes they have granted.
They look on everyone as blessed.

Their sweet innocence.
Always brings Mother Nature's presence.
She loves them with a mother's desire.
The angels sing their praise,
In the heavenly choir.

Lady of the Lake

Lady of the lake.
Lady of fantasy.
You held the sword of destiny.

Beauty knows your name.
You are a goddess without shame.

With your armour of heavenly light.
It shines in the moonlight.

Your home is Avalon.
A magical kingdom.
A place of hope and freedom.

To Avalon,
We shall go.
To a place only heaven knows.

Moon of Love

In a beautiful night.
The moon of love shines with angelic light.

Angels of heaven,
Watch over it with loving prayer.
When love is in the air.

The moon of love,
Is full of happiness.
When love is there,
There is no sign of sadness.

Winters Storm

Under my duvet,
Nice and warm.
I can hear the Winters storm.

I can hear the howling wind,
As I pull my duvet to my chin.
I am cosy and warm tonight.
Now I wish to say,
Goodnight!

Excalibur

Sword of destiny,
Your name will live on.
In legend and beyond.
You were forged at Avalon.

From a rock,
Destiny brought you a man.
Together,
You will build a kingdom which would stand.

You stood for chivalry and nobility.
You brought knights to a table of purity.

When the tale began to break.
Excalibur was returned to the lake.
The Lady of the lake took it by the hand,
And took it into the depths away from mankind.

The Lady of the lake took the sword,
For King Arthurs sake.
His dying wish,
Was for the sword to be returned to whence it came.
A sword with a powerful name.